Also by Suzen Fromstein

SUITS AND LADDERS
Ten Proven Ways to Keep Your Job Safe
(with a few jokes thrown in)

A unique, easy to read and often humorous
corporate survival guide based on the combined
wisdom of 102 real people with real jobs

(in progress)

Killers, Coffins & Cadavers
A Humorous Guide to Death & Dying
(co-authored with Elaine Smookler and
Michael Nemiroff)

3

Dedication and Acknowledgments

This book is dedicated to my two amazing sons Mikel and Dustin Fromstein and to Michael Nemiroff and Elaine Smookler. You make me laugh. You make me cry. You make me grow. For that I am eternally grateful.

Special thanks to my son Mikel for his amazing cover design and print layout, to my friends Al Emid, Cameron Freeman and Grant Lee for their unwavering encouragement and moral support, to my dear friend and cheerleader Shirley Crockett who edited this work and to Donna Carrick and Carrick Publishing who e-published it.

> BONUS: HOW TO ADD HUMOR TO EVERYTHING
> *Co-authored with Stand-up Comic MICHAEL NEMIROFF*

SUZEN FROMSTEIN

WANT TO INFORM, INFLUENCE AND ENTERTAIN LIKE A PRO?

SIMPLY RECOGNIZE THE SEVEN DEADLY SINS OF PUBLIC SPEAKING AND THEN AVOID THEM

WANT TO INFORM, INFLUENCE AND ENTERTAIN LIKE A PRO?
Simply Recognize The Seven Deadly Sins of Public Speaking And Then Avoid Them
by Suzen Fromstein

BUSINESS / HUMOR / PERSONAL GROWTH
ISBN: 978-0-9881515-1-2
The Write Connections Inc.
suzen@suzenfromstein.com
416-471-3845

TABLE OF CONTENTS

THE SEVEN DEADLY SINS OF PUBLIC SPEAKING

Compares and contrasts Peak and Weak podium
performances, more embarrassing moments, rules of
thumb from Toastmasters, pros and cons of PowerPoint
presentations, when and how to use Handouts and the
foibles of prepared introductions, + more, more, more

INTRODUCTION

Good presentation skills can help you in all aspects of your personal and professional life including:

- Convincing your partner to spend money on a new 52" 3D TV rather than on that dream vacation she had her heart set on.

- Having the last word in an argument about who comes first in your relationship, as if he didn't know; and, most importantly.

- Helping you engage upper management long enough to absorb the merits of your process innovation or cost saving idea.

The majority (ninety percent) of the mid-to-senior level managers I interviewed for SUITS AND LADDERS: Ten Proven Ways to Keep Your Job Safe (with a few jokes thrown in) identified presentation and public speaking skills as one of the top ten corporate survival strategies. They also said that formal public speaking training delivered an immediate and measurable return on their investment of time and money.

Nerves, feelings of embarrassment and self-doubt (more formally called performance anxiety) often get in the way of a peak performance. In the not-so-distant-past, I compulsively prepared and practiced for as long as forty hours for one five-minute address.

Through trial and error I became aware of the Seven Deadly Sins of Public Speaking and then I learned how to Avoid Them. This gave me the confidence to compete on the Toastmasters stage, to teach Effective Business Presentations at a local community college, to write executive speeches and to run business workshops and seminars (attended by 750 people at the same time). I wrote this book to summarize what I have learned from both sides of the podium.

THE
SEVEN
DEADLY
SINS
OF
PUBLIC
SPEAKING

Sin #1:
Failure To Practice
Properly – Or At All

Believe it or not, the more intelligent the speaker, the more likely he or she is to wing it. Since you are so smart, brilliant even, you probably neglect to practice at all, or to practice enough before your public appearances. Mistake.

Your job as a speaker is to engage, challenge and entertain your listeners. They will respect you even more when you do all three. At the very least, your audience expects you to be familiar with your material, the equipment, and how to pronounce names and terms. Let's face it, some words are "downrightchthonic" to pronounce.

Your audience wants to see and hear a professional performance and expects your remarks (and your shoes) to be polished. They are also so grateful it is you up there instead of them that they are prepared to cut you a little slack. But, their gratitude only buys you a "get out of jail card" for about three or four minutes. After that, their patience and their attention span, leaves the building. Prepare first and foremost by rehearsing your remarks.

If you fail to practice (out loud, not in your head), you tell your listeners that your time is more important than theirs.

Remember, if you are representing your company, your employer has probably spent thousands of sponsorship and advertising dollars securing the speaking slot for you.

You have to practice if you want to maximize the return on your organization's investment of its resources. Ask yourself if you and your company can bear the consequences of a weak performance. If the answer is 'No' then allocate enough time to practice or find someone else to deliver your remarks.

If failure to practice properly is the sin, what is the salvation?

Be prepared to put in some serious practice time. I usually budget one hour of preparation (research, theme development, writing the speech script and practicing) for each one minute of presentation. For example, a thirty-minute speech requires thirty hours of preparation. If someone else is doing the research and writing the script, cut your preparation time in half.

There are a number of proven practice techniques at your disposal:

- Seek out all internal and external speaking opportunities. Every hour of stage time increases your self-confidence.

- World Class Speakers like Dale Carnegie have "mirrored" their way to speaking success. You can too. Practice your speech 3 to 7 times in front of the mirror. This provides immediate, visual feedback on what the audience sees. Mirror practice allows you to identify what to change. Make these modifications and then practice your revised script another 3 to 7 times.

- Learn how to use the technology you are depending upon and have someone with you who knows how it works. Be prepared for the technology to fail and your assistant to get the flu. Get to know your material cold. This investment of time will increase your confidence and help you survive any technological malfunctions.

- Tape record and videotape your practices. Replay the recordings. What did you like? What needs to be changed? What words were hard for you to say? Make the changes and then listen to the new recordings. Keep doing this until you are satisfied with the result. Get rid of every word that does not contribute to the idea at hand.

- Then, tape record and videotape all of your live performances.

- Always solicit anonymous feedback from audience members. Your friends, your romantic partner and the people who report to you may not tell you if your content, information flow and delivery are on point. And, your mother just might be a bit biased, so take her compliments like you take her gravy, with a pinch of salt.

Independent audience feedback identifies areas for continued improvement. And, whenever you are asked to provide comments on another speaker's performance, please take the time to do so.

Sin #2:
No Well-Defined Theme

Some speeches have no unifying theme or try to cover too
many topics and ideas. Others say nothing of value or try to
say too much. None of these approaches are effective. Just
like failure to practice, the absence of a well-defined theme
suggests the audience is not important to the speaker, or
even worse, that the ideas are not important.

Example of a Well-Developed Theme

Several years ago I visited a butterfly farm in the Caribbean.
Although I thought the many multi-coloured species were
beautiful, even five minutes later, I could not recall any of
their names. I can however, repeat the guide's lecture almost
verbatim. That is because of his choice of theme, namely that
human males and male butterflies are essentially the same.

Since my mind, my curiosity and my sense of humor were
engaged by the theme, I listened intently to everything the
guide said. Even today, I have perfect recall of every juicy
bit of his lecture. Here's what the guide said.

"When the male butterfly emerges from his chrysalis, he
looks for the nearest open bar. In nature, the open bar

consists of flowers and rotting fruit that have fallen onto the ground, because both have an extremely high sugar and alcohol content.

When the male butterfly is totally drunk, he is ready for the main event - anonymous sex with a willing female. He dances erratically in an open field, hoping his gymnastics will be an appropriate aphrodisiac. A few males actually find the female butterfly of their dreams. Most however, are eaten by the birds.

Contrast the fun life of sex, drugs and rock and roll enjoyed by every male butterfly with the life of drudgery and toil experienced by the female butterfly. When she emerges from her chrysalis the first order of business is to find a male butterfly to father her children. Since all the male butterflies are pretty much pickled, she chooses the one less likely to bash them both into a tree.

The female butterfly initiates the sex act, and carries the co-joined couple through the air – the male butterfly is too drunk to do anything but just lie there. Their loving embrace ends when all of her 125 eggs are fertilized.

After the sex act, the two uncouple, and the male butterfly goes back to his buddies at the bar and the whole process starts all over again.

The female butterfly on the other hand must locate125 different leaves for each one of her fertilized eggs. She deposits one egg on the underside of each leaf. When she is finished her work she dies.

So it seems that the cute butterflies erratically lurching from flower to flower in your garden are only drunk males getting up the courage to entice a hardworking female to have sex with them."

I defy you to think of butterflies or bar hopping as you did before. That is the power of a well-defined theme.

If the absence of a well-defined theme is the sin, what is the salvation?

A perfect theme is the same as the perfect bumper sticker. Before writing your speech or presentation, identify the one message you want the audience to take home with them. Summarize it in one sentence - this is your theme.

Write your theme sentence on the top of a piece of paper. Every point in your presentation should then contribute to, enhance or illustrate your theme. When you establish a clear theme you automatically exclude any extraneous material.

Sin #3:
Failure To Focus On
Your Target Audience

I joined Toastmasters and earned my Competent Toastmaster
(CTM) and Advanced Toastmaster (ATM Bronze) credentials.
As I gained more confidence and experience, I realized that
my level of nervousness was directly connected to the script I
was writing in my head. In this script, I imagined the audience
was judging both my material and me. The moment I began to
focus on what my listeners required from me as a speaker, my
nervousness miraculously disappeared.

Every good speech is aimed at a specific segment of the
audience. These are the individuals who are able and willing
to respond to your central message. For example, to a
salesperson, the target audience consists of the people
who want or need the product being sold.

Personal Case Study 1:
A Not-So-Funny Speech Contest Entry

One year, I competed in the Toastmasters Humorous
Speech contest. I was convinced that my less-than-saintly
dating life was hysterically funny and would be the

winning competition entry. My target audience consisted of the Toastmasters in the audience and more importantly, the conservative judges.

No one was more surprised than I was when I placed a measly third. The first place entry was a boring speech about real estate and the second about the electrifying topic of financial planning.

I was completely shattered and I was confused - the audience had laughed so hard they had cried during my speech. They had not even chuckled during the other competition entries, including the first and second place winners.

After the shock wore off, and I took a little time to reflect, I realized my sin. Speaking about dating was more appropriate for a comedy club audience than it was for a Toastmasters audience, even in a humorous speech competition.

I had unknowingly committed the third deadly public speaking sin and neglected to focus on my target audience. Do you agree? My Toastmasters Humorous Speech Contest Script is included as Example 4 in the PUTTING THEORY INTO PRACTICE section.

Personal Case Study 2: But, I already know that

I recently volunteered to be part of a peer-judging panel. My fellow judges and I had been accredited for at least five years. We were responsible for conducting the oral portion of an accreditation exam. Our job was to ask the candidates a series of prepared questions on current events, ethics, and professional practice (sounds oddly like the questions asked by a hiring manager during a job interview).

All judges were required to participate in a mandatory 45-minute orientation webinar. The organizer wasted the first twenty minutes talking about why accreditation was important. I was bored stiff. As mentioned earlier, I was already accredited and understood the process. Had my participation not been mandatory, I would have logged off.

After about twenty minutes, the organizer finally got around to telling me what I needed to know as an oral examiner. By failing to focus on her audience (the volunteer judges), the organizer wasted time telling me what I already knew. This left a bad taste in my mouth and diminished my positive feelings about the whole judging experience.

If failing to focus on your target audience is the sin, what is the salvation?

Understand your presentation purpose. Is your talk supposed to persuade or convince the audience to take action? Is it focused on providing information? Or are you just there to entertain them? If so, don't forget your unicycle.

Identify and profile your target audience. Age? Gender? Income? Occupation? Education? Lifestyle? Do they have any of each?

Make some reasonable guesstimates about the audience's familiarity with and level of knowledge of the subject matter. This allows you to limit the time you spend on developing these points.

What is their relationship to you and to each other? What do they have in common with each other? What are their issues, concerns and "hot" buttons? Are they for or against your position?

Identify WIFM – what's in it for me (also known as why should I stop tweeting or updating my Facebook status and listen to you?). Figure out what your audience is looking for and identify why you are the right person to deliver the message. Then deliver it. In return your audience will give you their time, their attention and their respect.

Sin #4:
Lack Of Passion

A speech without passion is a speech without power. Take a clear stand on a subject about which you feel strongly. Sincerity and enthusiasm are required before you can engage and mobilize any audience, especially a skeptical business audience.

As partners, your words, your voice and your body work together. They tell the audience if you are happy to be there, if you believe in what you are saying, if you are confident and in control, and if you are interested in, and care about them. Don't be afraid to use humor to break up the mind-numbing flow of data.

Let's start with the words you use. Educators believe that people employ three primary learning styles when they consume and respond to information. Visual learners run a movie or see a picture of the information in their minds. Audio learners rewind the tape and listen to what was said or how the information sounded. Kinesthetic learners process data by feeling, playing or working with it.

Everyone can and does process data using all three learning styles. When you speak and write, use words from all three learning styles rather than restrict your vocabulary to only appeal to the visual learners in the audience. That way, you will touch upon how everyone in the audience consumes information. Here are some examples of words from the three different learning styles I used in this book:

Visual

- slimy frog
- like a shield
- use your mouth energetically
- throw your words
- hot buttons
- I picked Playboy
- I would have ordered KFC

Audio

- incessant throat clearing
- a monotone speech pattern
- pitch is too low
- a conversational tone
- avoid shouting
- help your body speak
- harsh tones
- crinkling paper

Kinesthetic

- passionate speech
- imagine how your audience feels
- heated debate
- refreshing noon nap
- I wanted a man
- reflect your feelings
- search your heart
- one day the Maple Leafs will win the Stanley Cup (it wasn't really in the text, I just wanted to see if you were paying attention).

And, if you want to cover all of your bases, you can also enliven your material with some olfactory (smell) and gustatory (taste) words.

Olfactory

- pass the smell test
- rotten in Denmark
- sweet smell of success
- new car smell
- smell of fresh baked bread
- bad breath

Gustatory

- bad taste in my mouth
- in good taste
- spicy
- flavorful
- mouth watering

Your voice

A good speaking voice will help you:
- get recognized and promoted at work
- make sales
- win respect
- improve your social opportunities, and,
- speak effectively to audiences.

Remember, there is no place for poor breathing patterns and harsh tones in a passionate speech or a heated debate. Your listeners make assumptions about your personality, intellect, emotional state, attitudes, and trustworthiness based solely upon your voice.

For example, if you speak in a monotone or if your pitch is too low, people will assume you are bored, unmotivated, unintelligent and unprepared. If you use too high of a pitch, people will think you are out of control, hysterical, immature, uncertain, or all of the above.

Many public figures understand the importance of a good speaking voice. Margaret Thatcher, a female Prime Minister of the United Kingdom (1979-1990) lowered her voice timber because she wanted to be taken more seriously by her male colleagues and constituents.

When you use a lot of fillers (uh, er, um, you know, like), or if every statement sounds like you are asking a question, people will believe you are uncertain or untrustworthy. I once had a colleague that said, "You know what I mean" after every other sentence and another who apologized all the time. Their use of fillers was annoying and more importantly didn't reflect their level of knowledge, skills or professional abilities.

Don't use "OK" or "right?" at the end of a sentence. The expression sounds too aggressive. Use a conversational tone when speaking in public. Project your voice but avoid shouting. If you are too loud, people will believe that you are out of control. Use your mouth energetically. Throw your words out to the laps of the audience.

Body language

Your physical appearance strongly influences how people judge you. Unless you are auditioning for a makeover show, you have a specific age, height, weight, and facial characteristics. You can enhance these aspects with proper business attire, grooming and physical conditioning. Body language is so important when speaking.

American essayist, lecturer and poet Ralph Waldo Emerson (1803-1882) said, "What you do speaks so loud that I cannot hear what you say." Contemporary communications experts agree with Emerson. Some say that more than half of communication comes from body language and about a third from the speaker's tone of voice. Others suggest that over ninety percent of communication is nonverbal. The speaker's words account for less than ten percent of communication. In other words (did you catch that unintended pun?), most communication takes place on a nonverbal level.

Effective presentations involve the whole person and your body helps you make (as well as score) points. You can help your body speak by ridding yourself of any distracting mannerisms, giving it permission to reflect your feelings, being natural and conversational, and building self-confidence through preparation.

Your body language adds punctuation to your material and makes the information more meaningful and memorable for the audience. It is perfectly acceptable to gesture as long as the movements clarify and support your words, dramatize your ideas, function as a visual aid, encourage audience participation, or dispel your own nervous tension.

The body language of the individuals in your audience will tell you if they are engaged and actively listening to you. You are in good shape if most of your audience members are sitting on the edges of their seats, slouching, with slightly tilted heads, have at least one hand on one part of the head, and they are stroking their face or pulling on their beards and mustaches, especially the men.

If most of the heads are not tilted, your business audience has stopped listening to you. Be prepared to do something differently if all you see are:

- crossed arms and legs combined with buttoned coats/jackets

- frowns and angry looks

- previously tilted heads become erect

- slouchers acquire straight backs

- audience members are looking at the ceiling/their watches/their phones/each other

- their bodies are actually pointing towards the door because they can hardly wait to get out of there

- continuous shifting of bodies

- nonstop throat clearing

- closed/hooded eyes (with a large percentage of sleepwalkers advancing toward the stage).

A Not-So-Personal Case Study

Here's how a client joked about body language in his speech on explaining poor performance.

"At various times in my professional career, I have had to respond to negative feedback on the spot. For example, once, a performance measurement consultant presented my client's investment committee with a lengthy and damning portrait of the reasons for our poor investment performance. This resembled a dissection in high school biology class, and I was the slimy frog.

The consultant's analysis was detailed and right on the mark. When he had finished he left. The room was silent. I felt that everybody was waiting for my response.

I took a deep breath and said 'Well, that was very interesting' and all of my clients' heads nodded in agreement. 'And,' I continued, 'To be frank, the consultant said so much I am not quite sure what to make of it all.' To my delight all the clients' heads nodded again.

Suddenly I realized that their heads were nodding because they were sleeping. The consultant's long and boring presentation had put them into a coma! They hadn't heard a word he or I had said. He saved my neck!

Seriously, the lesson here is that I wasn't there to refute the consultant's analysis or to make excuses for my poor performance."

Personal Case Study 3:
A Large Percentage of Sleepers May be Nothing More Than a Bunch of Tired People

I once delivered a noon presentation to some primary school teachers. I was a seasoned speaker by then and was suitably horrified when eight out of the ten teachers in my audience nodded off during my prepared remarks. I later learned that the sleeping teachers used their lunch hour to take a refreshing noon nap. This helped them recover from the rigors of the morning. The fact that any of them stayed awake during my remarks was a testament to my presentation skills and abilities.

Timing or pace

Timing or pace is the rate at which you deliver your sentences and ideas. Too quickly says you want to get through the presentation as fast as possible. Too slowly appears condescending or suggests that you don't know what's coming next.

Pause after you make an important point to let it sink in or after you ask a rhetorical question. This gives audience members an opportunity to answer your question in their minds, before you move them along.

If lack of passion is the sin, what is the salvation?

- Express, act out, demonstrate your passion and commitment to your message.

- Let your passion be your guide. If the message fails to excite you, imagine how your audience feels. Practice sparkling – just not too close to your BBQ. If your job requires you to give the speech, and there is no one else you can bribe to take your place, find something about the topic that excites you and go from there.

Sin #5:
Wasting The Opening

Individuals in the audience form their first impression of
who you are in the first four minutes. Some speakers waste
this time on mundane table talk. Others apologize for not
being prepared or tell unrelated genie jokes.

To Inform, Influence and Entertain Like a Pro you have
to engage the audience. How do you do this effectively?
Ask a question or deliver a startling statement or statistic.

Then pause for a second to give the audience a chance to
absorb what you have said or to answer your question(s)
in their minds. Don't rush into the next sentence.

The same goes for laughter. After you have delivered a
great punch line and there is laughter, don't try and speak
over the laughter. Wait until the audience has stopped
laughing before you continue speaking.

Examples of Good Opening Lines

In this introduction from a speech I delivered to a business
audience on Robert Kiyosaki's book I purposefully started
with a provocative statement.

"Be good." "Study Hard." "Get Good Grades."

"Why?" the child asks his mommy.

"So you can get a good job," she replies.

Ladies and Gentlemen:

"If you want to be rich and happy don't go to school," says Robert Kiyosaki in his book with the same title. He contends that our education system is really an employment process that is not designed for learning, but is rooted in the fear of not earning."

Were they listening? You bet they were!

Personal Case Study 4: The Rules Apply Even If You Aren't The Only Speaker

I was recently a member of a panel of experts invited to speak to financial executives about reinventing their careers after fifty. The moderator gave each panelist three minutes to introduce himself or herself.

Because I wanted to establish rapport quickly I opened with a hard-hitting and extremely relevant question. I asked, "Are you prepared to be fired?"

Then I paused for the length of time it took to say "one steamboat." The pause gave audience members time to reflect on my question. I then answered the question, "I wasn't." These few words established me as someone with a perspective about reinventing a career after fifty. The audience was engaged and more importantly listening.

If wasting the opening is the sin, what is the salvation?

- Start strong. Leap right into your speech. Remember, it is never necessary to recover from a great beginning.

- A question or a sobering statistic will spark the audience's attention.

- Create a positive first impression and the audience will not only be on your side, they will stay there.

Sin #6:
A Weak Close

You have to ask for the job, the opportunity, or the date. Your concluding remarks are the most important part of your presentation and I'll prove it to you. Ask yourself if you would rather have the first word in an argument or the last? Now you know why your closing remarks are so important.

Good Closing Lines

In my Toastmasters humorous speech contest entry (PUTTING THEORY INTO PRACTICE Example 4) I spent the entirety of my speech entertaining the audience with the gory details of my love life.

By the time the speech ended I met someone. Even with his many flaws and the hilarity of the search, the audience was relieved that I finally got a date. Although I could have ended there I wanted to close my humorous speech with a laugh. Read Example 4 to determine if I met my objective.

Does this theory work on speeches that deal with more intellectually stimulating subjects? Absolutely! The goal of my speech was to inspire my audience to think about our education system differently. Here's how I ended my speech on Robert Kiyosaki's views about our education system:

> "How would Christopher Columbus have fared in today's educational system? Kiyosaki contends he would likely be labelled inattentive, a daydreamer or a disciplinary problem.
>
> If he was told to memorize a theory such as the earth is flat, Columbus would probably challenge it, only to have his teachers and peers laugh at him for being so stupid.
>
> We are crushing today's Columbuses because students are not being taught how to think critically and independently.
>
> Isn't it contradictory that we have a system of education that promotes Christopher Columbus as a courageous hero, yet punishes students for having original ideas, taking initiative and making mistakes?
>
> Kiyosaki asks us to consider what is more important. The year 1492 or the fact that a dreamer named Columbus challenged current wisdom – that the earth was flat - and had the courage to raise money and take a mutinous crew to the edge of the earth?
>
> Isn't it time we ask ourselves if we are on the ship with the new Columbuses or standing on the shore heckling them?"

If a weak close is a sin, what is the salvation?

- Write the conclusion first. This is your most powerful point.
- You are the expert. It is unnecessary to thank your audience for listening to you.

Sin #7: Failing To Write The Speech Script

The smarter a speaker is, the higher the likelihood he or she will try to work from weak notes, improvise or fake it. In the absence of a script: the speaker talks too long on one thing and not long enough on another; key points are omitted; and the speaker loses track of the time and the point is lost to say nothing of boring repetition, repetition, repetition.

The rule of three

If you can remember the number three you can write and deliver an effective speech or presentation. Since people rarely retain any more than three pieces of new information at one time, only focus on three main ideas.

Luckily for us, there are also three structural elements of a speech (open, body, close), the three delivery mechanisms (words, body and voice) and the three prerequisites for success (research, preparation and practice).

Open, body, close

Your opening statement tells the audience what you want them to think about. The body of your presentation includes information about that subject that is important. Your closing statement loops back to the opening statement, summarizes your key points and includes your call to action.

Think triple layer pastrami sandwich and you'll have it right. In the sandwich approach, you tell the audience what you are going to tell them – that is your opening. Then you tell them (the three points you have developed in the body of your speech). And then you tell them what you told them – this is your close. Whether you are giving a professional speech, a business presentation, or a toast to the bride, to be effective, all three structural elements are required.

If failing to write the speech script is a sin, what is the salvation?

1. For twenty minutes, write down everything you can think of that deals with your topic. Then, put it away.

2. Review these ideas a day or two later. Add relevant material to them.

3. What's your main point (theme)?

4. Write your theme sentence on the top of a blank sheet of paper. Copy the ideas from items 1 and 2 under your theme sentence.

5. What point belongs first? Second?

   Speech Writer's Rule: open your speech with the second most important point and close with your most powerful point.

6. Write down examples, evidence and reasoned argument that support each point of the speech.

   Speech Writer's Rule: no more than three powerful points. All examples should support these three points.

7. Write your speech script from these notes.

   Speech Writer's Rule: Write the conclusion first.

8. Find a writing buddy. Have them critique your script. Listen to them.

9. Talk your speech script into a tape recorder. Play it back. While listening to your recording, write in any needed changes.

10. Practice 3 to 7 time in front of the mirror. Give it everything you've got. Clean mirror afterwards.

11. Make any needed changes. Repeat steps 8 and 9 as needed.

12. Thrill the audience with your speechmaking prowess.

PLUS • PLUS • PLUS •

A Peak and a Weak Performance

We have all sat through lackluster, boring, irrelevant, and coma-inducing business presentations. Far too many business speakers cram so much data into their speeches and presentations that they suffocate the audience's minds, along with their own credibility (I call this data dumping). The differences between a Peak and a Weak performance are listed below:

Peak

- KISSS
(keeps it short, simple and specific by):
- being accurate and concise
- using vocal variety and being animated
- varying the pace and maintaining eye contact
- including interesting visuals
- focusing and organizing your remarks
- having fun
- encouraging audience participation
- being innovative and doing something different
- dressing appropriately

Weak

- KILL

(kills the audience's interest by):
- being unfamiliar with the material
- reading the PowerPoint slides
- not varying the sentence length
- no enthusiasm
- visuals have no meaning
- boring/too technical
- doesn't engage the audience
- speaker is over/under dressed

Personal Case Study 5: Say It Don't Spray It

I once was in charge of promoting an upcoming conference. I indulged in the veggies and dip about a half hour before I was scheduled to go on stage. Although I had brushed my teeth, I still managed to spray the front row with bits of carrot, broccoli and celery while demonstrating my passion for my message. Although most of them were surprised one person did exclaim, "Great Waldorf."

Toastmasters Rules of Thumb

- Be at least as well dressed as the best-dressed person in your audience. Unless you are using your clothing as a prop, save the low cut tops, torn jeans and flip-flops for the weekend. Birkenstocks are not formal dress except in Portland.

- Ensure that every item of clothing is clean, well tailored and well fitting. Jewelry that glitters or jingles when you move or gesture diverts attention. Empty your pockets of bulky objects or coins that produce audible sounds when you move. And, speaking of pockets, keep your hands where your audience can see them.

- Audiences like speakers who radiate good health and physical vitality, and who look good. As per Personal Case Study 5, be mindful of what you eat before you go on stage.

PowerPoint

Unless I am delivering a webinar, I don't use PowerPoint for one important reason – I don't want anything to get between my audience and me. When I'm working the technology, I am focused on when the next slide is coming up. When I don't use PowerPoint I am focused on the audience. If you still are not convinced and would prefer to use PowerPoint, please use a remote clicker.

One of the reasons PowerPoint is so popular is because it allows the presenter to disseminate a lot of technical information relatively quickly and taps into both oral and visual learning styles.

Some business speakers make the mistake of including their entire speech script in their PowerPoint slides. PowerPoint contains a "Notes" section that only the presenter can read. Please cut your speech script into the Notes section.

Do not try and cram everything onto the one slide. Let the information breathe and speak for itself. Only use three or four bullet points per slide and three or four words per line. Don't be afraid to include graphics, pictures, or cartoons in your PowerPoint slides. Be especially diligent in terms of copyright issues.

Without exception, Do Not read your slides. One of the 102 real people with real jobs that I interviewed for SUITS AND LADDERS said it best, "There is nothing worse than watching someone read his or her PowerPoint slides. You shouldn't have to look at the slide to figure out what to say. You only inspire trust and confidence if you don't read your slides."

Handouts

Do not give the audience your speech script when they enter the room – give it to them when they leave. Why should I bother to listen to you if I have everything in front of me? When you give me something to read that is exactly what I'm going to do. What part of reading has to do with listening to you? With your script in front of me I'm also tempted to correct your grammar, spelling mistakes and pronunciation errors.

Formal Introductions

When someone introduces you, he or she establishes you as an authority on the topic and gets the audience excited about all the wonderful things you are about to tell them. However, don't make the mistake I made and assume that the person making the introduction is familiar or comfortable with their role.

I recommend that you talk to the person who is introducing you beforehand. Find out his or her comfort level with making a formal introduction. Maybe he or she would prefer it if you introduced yourself.

Personal Case Study 6:
Introductions can turn an audience from neutral to hostile

I was invited to speak about how to write a winning proposal. Unfortunately, I assumed that the executive director of the professional association would be comfortable delivering my prepared introduction. After all, he hired me!

Before he called me to the podium, the executive director read my prepared introduction. Unfortunately for me, he added, "I'd like to read the introduction that Suzen Fromstein prepared for herself."

With these few words the executive director killed my credibility. Although I recovered by the end of the workshop, I had to fight hard to earn the audience's respect and trust. I wouldn't have had to work so hard if I had established his comfort level in advance or had a prepared comeback.

For example, I might have said, "Your reading was so spectacular that I can hardly wait to hear everything that I have to say!"

Prepare and practice comebacks for a bad introduction, equipment malfunctions, lost handouts, forgetting where you are in the script etc. That way you will be prepared if something like this happens to you.

Audience Q&A

If your session has a question and answer component at the end, have one or two prepared questions ready. For example, you might say, "A question I'm often asked is…." Then answer it. If there are still no questions, you could say, "Another question, I'm often asked is…" Then answer that question (please see Example 1 of PUTTING THEORY INTO PRACTICE for an example of two prepared questions that related to the speaker's remarks).

Or, you can always have someone you know in the audience ask a prepared question. That way you will avoid the dead air space that can occur when there are no questions from the audience especially when the agenda calls for a five or ten minute Q&A.

Rather than just thanking the audience for listening to you, use the opportunity to remind the audience of your three key points. Never end your speech or presentation with the Q&A.

The More Advanced Speaker

Since I wanted to be a great speaker, I searched for ways to get the focus away from my shaky knees and upset stomach and put it where it belonged - on the audience. "Experiential Education" was the key.

Experiential education establishes rapport between the speaker and the audience. Once rapport has been established people are usually more willing to listen to what the speaker has to say. Since I stumbled across this key I have discovered a number of ways to use experiential education in my business speeches.

Intention Statement

I begin all of my public training seminars with my intention statement. This gives me an opportunity to outline what information I will be covering and what the audience can expect (tell them what I'm going to tell them).

It also takes the pressure off of me as the speaker and puts the emphasis where it belongs - on the audience. As the speaker, I am simply a conduit for the information.

I don't stop with my own intention statement. In order to neutralize the feelings, issues and circumstances audience members had when they took their seats (e.g. if they had a fight with their significant other, were worried about an upcoming crucial conversation or just needed a nature break) I ask audience members to take a minute and write down their intention statement for the session.

If I notice the audience does not appear to get what I'm asking them to do, I am ready with some examples.

- what do you want to accomplish, learn from me or from each other or receive during the limited time we will be together?

Crafting an intention statement often neutralizes the feelings, issues and circumstances that came into the room with the participants. More importantly, my speech, lecture, or training session becomes intensely personal for everyone in the room.

Let Your Audience Talk

Another way to have your audience "experience" your speech is to allow them to interact with each other. This is especially effective for a session that will last longer than an hour and takes the pressure off of the speaker to talk for the whole time.

Although many people are shy and feel uncomfortable talking in front of a large group, they are usually willing to talk with other table members or to one other person. I often ask audience members to say their names, company names and positions and their intention for the session out loud to at least one other person in the room.

Different Room Configurations

If your audience is sitting at round tables, designate one person at each table to be the first speaker. Only one person should be talking at any given tine. When that person has finished speaking, the next person at the table can talk and so on.

If a particular table is finished before the rest of the room and provided everyone has had a turn to say something, table members can talk quietly among themselves, until the facilitator closes the intention statement component of the workshop.

If on the other hand, the room is set up in a traditional lecture style, with rows of chairs, one row can turn and face the other row or the person on the left can talk to the person on the right. The interesting thing about an exercise of this sort is that it shifts the energy in the room. Audience members are forced to engage when they talking!

Make It Personal

Although every speaker's worst nightmare is losing control of the room, talking and even movement are two wonderful ways to ensure audience members are engaged. If you are fairly confident that all audience members don't know each other, you may want to try this technique:

Have everyone stand up and meet five people in the room they don't already know. Like the earlier exercise, each person can state their name, company name, their position and their intention statement. After he or she has listened to the other person give the same information, business cards can be exchanged. Then it is time to move on to four different people. When the process has been completed five times, the participants can return to their seats.

Play Games

Another effective way to have your audience experience your speech is to have them play a game related to the point you are trying to make. Many sophisticated speakers design their own games. If you choose to go this route, make sure that you test your game on a live audience before you incorporate it.

Personal Case Study 7: Buddy Up

Recently I had occasion to speak to a group of women entrepreneurs. At the onset, I separated friends who had come to my session together. I did not want to be dealing with any cross talk during my workshop. To address this without insulting audience members, I had everyone in the room look around and see if there was at least one other person they did not know. If they knew everyone, who was the person they knew the least or wanted to get to know better.

I also told the audience that under no circumstances could they choose the person with whom they came into the room. When they received the instruction to do so, they were to walk over to the person they had chosen, and tell that person they wanted to work with them for the balance of the workshop.

If that person was already spoken for, they were to go to the next person on their list and so on. Whenever there are an odd number of participants, you can always make a "triad" (a group of three people rather than two people).

It is critical that your instructions are clear if you want audience members to do something. I learned this the hard way. I keyed up the buddy exercise (as described previously). Except I neglected to tell participants what to do when they found their buddies. This meant I had thirty rather loud buddy conversations going on at the same time. Although the audience was having a ball, I had lost control of the room.

Now what? I had some options. I could scream louder than everyone – but that is not very professional.

Instead, I chose to walk around the room to the various buddy couples and ask them if they had found their buddy. If they had made the appropriate connection, I told them to sit down and continue their conversation quietly from their seats. This worked like a charm. Audience members never knew I had lost control of the room.

This situation provided me with a very valuable lesson. I learned I couldn't expect the audience to automatically know what I really wanted them to do unless I clearly spelled it out.

PUTTING
IT
ALL
TOGETHER

Each year, business organizations spend hundreds of thousands of dollars on town halls, client events, and seminars that fail to Inform, Influence or Entertain. No wonder companies have to bribe people to attend with food and drink.

In his play "No Exit" Jean Paul Sartre's three deceased characters are locked into a room together for eternity. This inspired the famous quote, "Hell is other people." It is within your power to save your audience from feeling similarly trapped. If you want to Inform, Influence and Entertain Like a Pro, Simply Recognize The Seven Deadly Sins of Public Speaking And Then Avoid Them!

BONUS: HOW TO ADD HUMOR TO EVERYTHING

(Including your business presentations)

by Suzen Fromstein and Stand-up Comic Michael Nemiroff

Shh – Your Audience is Sleeping

Whether you are pitching a new service to a customer, presenting your ideas to the boss or defending your poor performance to shareholders and other stakeholders, effective communication is essential.

This material is intended to be read by anyone who has ever given a sales report, market review, technical summary or conference presentation and found that his or her business audience was fast asleep, in a coma or dead.

If this has happened to you, it is likely because your presentation was meat-rich and sauce poor. Your remarks lacked the flavor and piquancy that metaphor, irony and humor bring to verbal communications (did you catch the metaphor at the end of the last sentence?). Everybody knows it yet nobody does it.

Why Aren't Business People Funny?

First, business people have tunnel vision when it comes to communicating in a business context. They think the bare facts are critically important and that any extraneous material is not, or even worse, is "inappropriate." They are wrong.

Adding material to spur the audience's interest in the subject at hand is extremely appropriate. Business folks speak in public because they want their audience to think about something in a new way or to take action like buy their product or service.

The speaker's job is to make sure the audience is awake and actively listening to the message. Only then can the audience absorb what you are trying to tell them and/or what you want them to do (your call to action).

Second, most business people regard humor and irony as a "lower" type of experience, rather undignified and entirely inconsistent with the aura and prestige of being "Sales Director of the Acme Whoopee Cushion Corp." Wrong again.

Your Lips are Moving and Nobody is Listening

…unless they are living with you or report to you. Seriously. Speech that triggers laughter (not at you, but with you) instantly transforms a talking head into an engaging human being that people want to listen to. By using humor appropriately, you are having a conversation. But this transformation is impossible when all you are doing is regurgitating key messages.

More importantly, a person who can make another laugh is seen to have power, intellect and charisma. And your potential clients and customers as well as your colleagues, boss, and Board:

- respect power,

- only listen to smart people, and

- want to hang out with people who are very good at what they do and entertain and amuse them.

For example, in pitching Montreal Quebec as a resource-rich environment to a group of potential clients, you could say:

> *"The fundamentals for solid economic growth in Quebec and especially in Montreal already exist. Montreal has a skilled labor pool with low mobility. Montreal has economic growth tied to the high tech*

industries. And Montreal has learned to combine
North American business sense with Latin thinking
and a French/European flair."

So far, so dull. But then you could add:

"So not only can you make money here, but we have
expanded the definition of allowable expenses to include
flamenco lessons, karaoke after dinner and free smokes
for everyone."

Suddenly you're funny and the audience is laughing with you
and more importantly, listening to you!

Although many business people know this is true, they still
can't write a speech with humor in it to save their lives,
never mind their jobs.

Let Me Entertain You

If you want people to pay attention to your sales pitch, make them laugh!

Advertisers use humor to bring their ideas to life in television commercials - and we all know that airtime is expensive. By making people laugh when they don't have to listen to you, they are more likely to stay engaged.

Here's an example. Recently, Moores Clothing for Men asked Canadians to donate gently used men's professional attire to help jobless men transition back into the work force.

We love everything about the Moores Suit Off Your Back campaign. It is for a great cause. The message is clever. And the male models aren't bad either.

In fact, if we had male partners, we would run (OK hobble) to the nearest Moores store and buy our special guys a whole new business wardrobe! So we know that humor works in advertising. But what about corporate communications?

Humor is a Powerful Communications Tool

There is absolutely nothing funny about failing to make your point, given the physical, mental, emotional and financial cost of making a mediocre speech or sales presentation.

Humor is an extremely powerful communication tool and can help you capture and keep the attention of your audience. Funny people put others at ease. Humor relaxes customers and makes them more receptive. Humor also may help distinguish you from your less amusing competitors.

Why Can't Business People Write Humor?

First, their egos. Everyone thinks he or she is funny. No hilarious. Just because you laugh at your own jokes, your staff laughs at your jokes and your partner laughs at your jokes, doesn't mean that you are funny.

The fact is, you have no sense of humor, your staff will laugh at anything you say, especially behind your back, and your partner is having an affair, and laughs at your jokes out of guilt. Very few people are naturally funny, at least not in any intellectual sense. Just listen to what people laugh at in bars or on television.

Relying on Your Improvisational Skills is Inviting Trouble

Second, business people won 't put in the work, don't have the time or can't see the benefit of making their boring PowerPoint slides entertaining.

Actually, the smarter people are, the more likely they are to improvise on the spot. And far too many believe that when necessary, they can easily dish out some delicious humor. However, unless you are Drew Carey or Robin Williams, relying on your improvisational comedy skills is inviting trouble, especially when it is really important that you make a good impression.

Humor is hard to write, especially effective humor. People who write jokes for a living know that, whereas people who don't write jokes for a living think humor and comedy writing is child's play.

Good Jokes Don't Grow on Trees

Many business people are now using classic joke writing techniques to bring business-appropriate humor to their articles, speeches and sales presentations.

All jokes require a "Set Up" followed by a "Punch." The Set Up is the smallest amount of information the audience needs to know or to guess what the joke is about. The Punch is the funny part. The funny part is only funny when people laugh.

Audience Members Typically Have Short Attention Spans

The trouble is, even when forced to sit down and focus, audience members typically have the attention span of a ferret on a double espresso. So, keep your Set Ups short and make sure your Punch isn't so obvious that the audience can see it coming.

In speechwriting, remarks that are surprising, off-beat, zany, absurd, even shocking or flat-out truthful, in respect to the Set Up, will elicit laughter from an audience. Here's a general example:

> **Set Up:** Five years ago my grandmother began walking five miles a day.

> **Punch:** Now we don't know where the heck she is!

The Punch is funny because it assumes that grandma didn't return home each day, but continued walking; so, of course, she's long gone. This is absurd, so it makes us laugh. As well, most people can't see this absurdity coming, so the Punch is also a surprise.

Working the Formula

Here's an example of some humor we created for a financial services client who was speaking to some financial advisors about the importance of customer contact during poor economic conditions:

Set Up: It is easy to make a client call when your performance numbers are up. It is extremely difficult to call on the same client when the numbers are down.

Set Up: Yet, client contact during poor performance periods is crucial to hanging onto the account. Even if it's the hardest thing you've ever done in your life, I urge you to continue to see clients, even if you only have bad news to impart.

Punch: You might say for example, "Good morning John. I'm here to report our computers crashed yesterday and converted all of your funds into Canadian Tire money. The good news is that Canadian Tire is up a point on the TSX."

Why this joke works: Here the joke is used to cushion the impact of the actual bad news and to lighten the context for the client.

Finally, there are styles, forms and formulas for crafting humor. Business people, to say nothing of the general public, haven't got a clue about them.

Here's another example of how we put this formula to work in a speech we wrote for one of our clients who delivered a business talk on the merits of buying real estate in Western Canada.

Set Up: The Western Canadian real estate story is truly amazing.

Punch: In fact, because Harper pulled Canada out of Kyoto, most of the western provinces will be beachfront in the future.

Why this joke works: In this example, the flat truth is a shock.

And, for his colleague who spoke on the merits of investing in Montreal, Quebec real estate:

Set-Up: Montreal is a world leader in special effects software for the motion picture industry. For example, blockbuster hits like "Titanic" and "Forrest Gump" were developed in Montreal.

Punch: Just don't blame the special effects industry for making Pauline Marois look good.

Why this joke works: In this example, there is a surprise addition of a political theme.

Blah. Blah. Blah.

The ability to make people laugh is a gift that needs to be shared, especially with those who don't know you are so superior. Just as it is important to know what to do, it is just as important to know what not to do.

Unfortunately, far too many corporate speeches and sales presentations overwhelm their audiences with facts and figures. And, it's difficult to create rapport with an audience of zombies.

As we noted in, "Sshh, Your Audience is Sleeping" speech that triggers laughter (with you, not at you) creates a new relationship between the speaker and the audience. Alas, too many speakers depend on fancy slide presentations to impress the audience. If, as Tom Stoyan, Canada's Sales Coach suggests, people buy people first, unless you are selling the technology, slick PowerPoint slides aren't enough to get you the sale or to convince anyone of anything.

As well, technology isn't always foolproof. Far too many times the equipment doesn't work well and/or the presenter has no clue how to operate it. So, it's better to rely upon a lively speech to impress people. If you must use technical equipment, memorize your remarks, so that you'll be prepared if the technology fails.

Mindless Data Dumping

This occurs when the bulk of your internal and external communications consists of paragraph after boring paragraph, of facts, figures, statistics and percentages. And data dumping will put your audience and your boss to sleep every time.

Personal Case Study 8: Too Much Information

There was a time when a subordinate asked me a question. Since I wasn't familiar with the file, I made the mistake of asking for a little background information. Silly me! I spent the next twenty minutes listening to so much detail (which included all the painful details of who said what to whom and when) that by the time my subordinate took a breath, I had forgotten my original question. What would have happened if my subordinate had to convince a divided and hostile board to vote in favor of a controversial motion?

What's the Alternative?

Use humor to break up the mind-numbing flow of data and to keep your audience (and your boss) awake. After every two or three technical points, punch the point home with a joke or humorous anecdote, as we did in this example from a speech about the merits of investing in Toronto.

> **Set Up:** Toronto is one of the strongest players in Canada because our economy draws its strength from a variety of the largest and fastest growing industry clusters. Let's look at some of these.

> **Set Up:** Financial, insurance and real estate – the Fire industries – represent almost one-third of Toronto's Gross Domestic Product.

> **Set Up:** The solid financial position of the major banks and the vigor of Toronto's real estate market will limit potential downswings in the Fire industries.

> **Punch:** And if anyone doesn't produce we Fire them!

> **Why this joke works:** Puns are typically a low form of humor. In this case the surprise is generated by the pun.

Although you can look to Google for inspiration, you will have to modify the humor so that it relates to your material. Too many speakers inject unrelated genie jokes into their corporate addresses. As you can see from the previous example, the material itself inspired the joke and we didn't have to pull any rabbits out of any hats either.

Flip-flops and Power Suits

Today's comedy club audiences like offbeat, inconclusive and morally ambiguous bits or routines focused on gross sex, defiance of authority and ambiguous morals. This formula not only gets you laughs, it may also get you your own show on the FOX Network.

However, a business venue is not a comedy club (even if it feels like one). Business speakers who take a comedy club approach run the risk of being seen as unprofessional – or worse.

The Good, the Bad and the Ugly of Self-Deprecating Humor

Self-deprecating humor is another risky proposition best used in internal business meetings or in situations where a personal relationship with audience members already exists. Self-deprecating remarks are a definite no-no in a public address to a room full of strangers, especially when you are trying to convince them to buy your product, service or idea.

Occasionally however, as you can see from the example taken from a speech we created for a senior commercial real estate sales executive on the merits of investing in Toronto, when used properly, self-deprecating humor can be effective.

> **Set Up:** Toronto's airport, Pearson International, is Canada's busiest airport and the 25th busiest in the world.

> **Punch:** In fact, we lose more luggage in one day than the rest of Canada loses all year!

Why this joke works: In this example, the self-deprecating pride in being incompetent, balances what some might perceive as an arrogant boast.

When is Irreverence Appropriate?

Irreverence can be very funny if carried out with tact and wit. Here's an example from a comedy show for the after-dinner entertainment of a group of financial advisors from the same company, both men and women.

Marketing material described the company's role in the financial planning process as that of a chief financial officer. Michael Nemiroff, who was the performer that evening, referred to the term and said that he guessed CFO meant, "See me, but if it doesn't work out, FO!"

Why this joke works: The deliberate misreading injected an improper but funny and surprising suggestion into the acronym.

Humor Sand Traps

Obviously, you'll want to avoid racist and sexist remarks as well as offensive references. Not sure? Ask!

Humor should always be appropriate to your topic and audience. For example, unless your speech to shareholders is on insider trading, livening it up with a joke about incest is not a good idea.

Beware of the language that looks appropriate when written into the speech script, yet sounds inappropriate when spoken aloud. Speechwriters must be sensitive to each speaker's normal tonal and pronunciation competencies. In order to determine whether the written words match the speaker, they must be spoken aloud, hopefully in front of the speechwriter who can make changes to the script before the speaker is embarrassed in public.

Vanilla Pudding or Cream Brule?

Advertisers use humor all the time. Business people don't use humor enough or at all. Yet humor is an extremely powerful business communication tool especially when there is negative information you want to convey.

That is because humor acts like a Trojan horse and fools the brain into thinking it's safe to receive the threatening message. Without humor, the brain shuts out the threatening information. Imagine the possibilities for corporate-appropriate humor when you have to deliver negative news or even any news more effectively.

But it is not appropriate to use humor to describe any situation that profoundly impacts life (e.g. business disasters or loss of life). It is also inappropriate to poke fun at specific individuals, unless it's at a roast or at a retirement party, where this type of humor is both appropriate and expected.

Language Creates Powerful Pictures

If your objective is to present yourself, your organization and your ideas with confidence, clarity and credibility, use language that creates powerful images. Humor will help you do this. Business speeches don't have to be dull and technical, but they often are because they restrict their language to business jargon.

Metaphors and Similes Add Color to Business Speak

Metaphors and similes liven up your presentation by providing images that are easier to recall than a series of technical facts. If you can make the occasional metaphor or simile comical the result can be especially effective workplace communication.

Here's a metaphor we created for one of our clients on the merits of investing in western Canada:

Set Up: Invest in Alberta oil.

Set Up: There is a helpful separation of provincial and federal interests.

Punch: All the oil is in Alberta, and all the dipsticks are in Ottawa!

Why this joke works: The insulting word "dipsticks" comes as a surprise in a sober Set Up.

And a simile we created comparing financial advisors to parents:

Set Up: You take care of other people's lives and are to be congratulated.

Set Up: Because you handle their money. I'm sure many of your clients are taken back to their teenage years when their parents controlled the cash.

Punch: I wonder whether any of your clients occasionally ask if they can borrow your car Saturday night?

Why this joke works: The absurd comparison of a financial advisor to a parent makes us laugh.

Your Mother Was Right – Practice Does Make Perfect

Timing, body language and vocal variety are all required to deliver humor effectively. Some speakers don't practice at all. Others don't practice enough. No wonder their podium performances are lackluster and forgettable.

If you can't afford the consequences of performing poorly, you can't afford to skip practice. If the speech doesn't warrant your serious preparation time, don't deliver it!

Treat Your Audience to a Banquet of Sights, Sounds and Stories

Even the most brilliant lines on the planet will not have the desired effect unless they are articulated clearly. You and only you, can make your words come alive.

There are subtle differences between the written and spoken word. You can't know how something sounds if you don't say it out loud. By definition, verbal communication requires you to actually say something (not just in your head).

Get your writing buddy or anybody you can take advice from without hating them (so forget your family) to critique your delivery, encourage you and give you honest feedback about your performance. Listen to them.

Practice in Front of the Mirror

When you have become comfortable with the script you and your writing buddy have worked on together, practice it for delivery and emphasis. That means you have to read it out loud.

The mirror is your best friend. You have to see what you look like when you are delivering the material because that is what your audience will see when they are listening to you.

Are you using your body to animate your words or are your hands just waving aimlessly like two sails? Are you smiling? Do you look as though you care about what you are saying? You won't be able to see what your audience sees unless you use the mirror (see discussion in Public Speaking Sin #1).

Tape record and/or videotape your practices (and all live performances). Replay the recordings. What did you like? Why? What needs to be changed? Make the changes and go back to the mirror and practice the changes.

We also recommend you solicit feedback from audience members on all live performances. Your mother's feedback doesn't count, but it's better than your brother-in-law's.

Ten Rules for Creating Powerful Humorous Moments

If you want to create some entertaining prose for your clients, colleagues and friends, we thought you might appreciate a quick summary of what you need to know.

1. Be prepared to put in some work – jokes are hard to write, especially good ones.

2. Don't try to be funny – remarks that are surprising, shocking, absurd, or even merely truthful will prompt laughter, especially if they seem to come naturally from the material.

3. Keep Set Ups short – Whether one person or several hundred, your audience has the attention span of a ferret on a double espresso. If you make them wait too long for the Punch, they will fall asleep!

4. Remember the Punches – at some point, you have to let the audience in on the joke.

5. Jokes on serious matters work - just remember rules 2, 3 and 4.

6. Expect nothing from your audience – that way you won't lose momentum or get flustered if they don't get it.

   Never apologize for the joke, even if it bombed. Don't bother to explain it. Just keep going. Maybe you surprised them and because they weren't expecting to hear a joke they weren't listening for one. They will probably laugh at the next one.

7. Even if you don't memorize your script, memorize all of your jokes, including the Set Ups and the Punch.

8. Find a writing buddy that you respect and trust (just don't lend them money). Don't be afraid to take his or her advice. If it makes comedic sense, use your writing buddy to help you rewrite your speech and to critique your performance.

9. Have fun with it – business speakers are not stand up comics. The good news is, your audience doesn't expect you to entertain them and will be very responsive when you make the effort.

10. Can't do it yourself? Hire a professional speechwriter! We happen to know two great ones.

There are also several useful books including any of the books by Gene Perrett and Judy Carter's Stand-up Comedy: The Book.

Toronto's Humber College runs a summer comedy writing and performance intensive where you can hone your skills or you can learn improvisational comedy techniques at Second City.

Toastmasters can help you with basic public speaking skills and there are Toastmasters Clubs in most areas of the world.

Follow our advice and humor will slowly creep into your consciousness and build a home there. Then you can visit it whenever you need to!

BONUS MATERIAL: PUTTING THEORY INTO PRACTICE

Actual Speech Scripts

Example 1: Explaining Performance and Rebalancing Strategies in a Difficult Market

Example 2: How to Hire a Money Manager

Example 3: Entertaining After Dinner Speech

Example 4: Suzen Fromstein's Toastmaster's Humorous Speech Contest Entry

BONUS
MATERIAL:
PUTTING
THEORY
INTO
PRACTICE

Actual Speech Script

Example 1: EXPLAINING PERFORMANCE AND REBALANCING STRATEGIES IN A DIFFICULT MARKET

Presented by the president of a money management firm to 150 institutional money managers.

"Good morning and welcome!

Before we begin, let me ask you two questions that form the basis of my talk today.

1. Have you ever had to deal with a really unhappy client?

2. As a result, have you ever lost an account that took a lot of time and money to develop because your client was disappointed with your performance or your service?

We've all thought about how to present "bad news" more effectively. Even if the client isn't particularly happy with your service or your performance, you want them to stay with you. Because we all know that it is more cost-effective in money management, as it is in matrimony, to hold onto our existing relationships, rather than find new ones.

Over the years, I have learned that presenting performance in context is particularly important during tough markets. In fact, what you present and how you present it, may determine whether an account continues or closes.

My speech today will focus on the "bad" times and I'll talk about how I deal with down markets and poor performance and still continue to get paid while most people get fired if that happens. For example, I recently learned that one of my company's major competitors, with a similar investment style to ours, has lost forty percent of its assets in the last eighteen months; our assets grew over this period!

As President and CEO it is up to me to hold the client's hand during "bad" times to ensure they stay with my firm. Besides which, if they do try to leave, I've still got them by the hand, which means, they're not going anywhere!

Seriously though. I don't believe any of us can afford to sit back and relax during the "good" times either. In fact, when the pressure to hold onto our existing accounts during the "bad" times eases, we are better able to improve our service and remove the minor irritants. And, if we don't, just watch how those "minor" irritants suddenly become "major" problems during periods of under-performance.

As a conference attendee, you will receive more than enough information on how to improve your strategies and systems from the other speakers. I plan to spend the next thirty minutes or so talking about what you can do when the client in the institutional marketplace is really irritated with you.

No matter how the markets are doing, but particularly when they are doing badly, the first thing we need to do is put ourselves in our clients' shoes and look at what it is like to do business with us, from their perspectives. It also helps to reflect on the level of service we, as consumers, expect to receive from our suppliers.

Over the years, I have delivered and received both "good" and "bad" service. And these personal experiences have shaped my understanding of what clients expect to receive from my firm. Here's what I mean.

My wife and I own a ski chalet in the U.S. I should note that we don't make it available to politicians for free!

A couple of years ago we decided to renovate the chalet. We hired a national building contractor who retained a local company to complete the renovation. As it turned out, we had major problems with this sub-contractor and it wound up costing us time and money. So we wrote to the contractor.

We were really impressed with his response. He came to see us in person on the weekend through several feet of snow. It was incredible! From a distance we thought it was Justin Trudeau trying to get our vote.

Before the contractor left, he asked us a very important question, "What can I do to make this better?"

My wife answered, "Don't charge us for the extra work."

He said, "OK."

Do you think we kept using this guy? Do you think we referred him to all of our friends? You bet we did!

Here's another example. Some years ago, when wearing a suit was mandatory for business people, I had to fly from Montreal to Vancouver. Unfortunately, I checked the suitcase that contained my only business suit. Naturally the airline lost it.

I awoke the next morning in Vancouver in a panic. No suit. No dress shirt. No tie. No shoes. Buying or renting replacement clothes was impossible because of my early morning appointment. And the entire look was much too Vancouver for me.

I called the concierge at the hotel. Within thirty minutes, he had found me a black suit, white shirt, black tie and black shoes. It was like magic! Mind you, I couldn't fit the top hat containing the rabbit into my briefcase, so I left them in the hotel room!

That quick-witted concierge salvaged my business trip with first-rate service. Would I suggest to my colleagues that they visit this hotel and ask for the concierge by name? Absolutely! And when you go, please tell him hello from the naked guy waving the business card.

Whenever I have to deal with an unhappy client, I take some time to think about my own personal experiences. These experiences shape what I say and do.

For example, four years ago I established XYZ Company as an investment counsellor in Canada. Because our portfolios are managed out of our head office in Europe, we had some issues with the timeliness and accuracy of our administration and reporting for our Canadian clients.

Customer complaints started to affect our reputation with prospective clients. And, finally it happened; a serious prospect chose not to do business with us after they checked our references.

I was furious – at myself. I reacted by sending a combined thank you and apology letter to the prospect that had rejected us and to the clients that had complained. Then I called all of our clients and told them they would not have to deal with these administrative issues again and that I would personally take whatever action was required.

Careers last a long time and the financial community in Canada is small. I wasn't going to damage my company's (or my own) reputation without a sincere, determined effort to fix things. As it turned out the cost of making the necessary improvements was negligible.

As you can see from the previous example, even administrative matters can lose business for you. The biggest problem however, is investment performance. If it persists, poor performance can trigger an effect I like to call the "vicious circle" or "tornado" or "there goes my year-end bonus."

Here's how it begins. Poor performance affects staff morale negatively and this worsens because of course, your customers aren't exactly thrilled with your poor performance either.

At a minimum, unhappy customers complain to you personally. Some go further and put sugar in the gas tanks of your company vehicles. This is especially bad for morale because no one can get home from the office at the end of a bad day!

Kidding aside, in the real world, what happens is that they fire you, which leads to even worse internal morale. Staff finds their customer relationships deteriorating faster and faster, accelerated by their own gloomy outlooks. You get the picture.

As President, it is my job to boost internal morale and to prevent our own people from developing gloom-and-doom attitudes, which ultimately affect the bottom line.

For example, after I left a former employer, the President unsuccessfully attempted to hang onto my clients. Since his company's investment performance was weak and had been weak for some time, his morale was low. When he visited my clients, he told them he didn't have any idea when things would improve and he wasn't sure what to do. He might as well have asked them straight out to fire him because that is exactly what happened.

Can you afford to have this happen to you?

If not, then you and your own people have to be prepared. Alert all of your people to specific client issues. If they believe they have addressed these concerns, ask them to prove their assertions to you.

It is easy to make a client call when your performance numbers are up. It is extremely difficult to call on the same client when the numbers are down. Yet, client contact during poor performance periods is crucial to hanging onto the account. Even if it is the hardest thing you've ever done in your life, I urge you to continue to see clients, even if you only have bad news to impart.

You might say for example, "Good morning John. I'm here to report our computers crashed yesterday and converted all of your funds into Canadian Tire money. The good news is that Canadian Tire is up a point on the TSX."

Before I enlarge upon how to present "bad" performance news in context, let's look at how clients react to weak performance.

Some clients begin to focus on absolute performance. Let's say for example, you are managing Canadian equities and the market is down five percent. All of a sudden, the original performance objective, which was to beat the Index by two percent goes out the window as the client starts to emphasize positive, absolute results. Some clients will even ask you to alter your investing style to respond to current market conditions.

And then there is the legalistic response that occurs when the client pulls out a poorly written contract that bases performance on a single time period.

Fishing expeditions are also typical and usually take the form of client requests for more data, more information and more meetings. As irritating as these reactions can be, remember, they come from your client's efforts to understand and maybe even reverse, an investment manager's underperformance.

As I mentioned earlier, it is possible, and in fact necessary, to respond to these types of concerns or you run the risk of losing the account. I'd now like to take the next ten minutes or so to talk about how I present information to clients that addresses underperformance issues.

The slide show is developed and presented to allay client concerns that we don't care or aren't aware of what's going on and to remind them about our strengths. It does not make excuses for poor performance. Whenever possible, the presentation seeks to re-establish trust and confidence by providing satisfactory explanations, not just excuses.

It is important to remember that the people you are presenting to are often required to explain or defend your underperformance to their colleagues. You may not be asked to attend these meetings, which means you may not be given another chance to elaborate upon any of your points. Your client presentations must therefore be clear, concise and easily explained by someone who may not have the same level of industry knowledge as do you.

By writing down the information in presentation format, the professional response, you can begin to remove the emotion ("You're losing my money hand over fist, you S.O.B.") and begin the process of rebuilding trust.

So what does this presentation look like?

The slides I will now show you are taken from an actual client presentation.

Slide 1:
I always begin my presentation with the conclusion and the things I want my client to remember. In fact, after going through the first slide, I often say, "and that concludes my presentation."

Slide 2:
Performance – in the case of this client, our last meeting was in November. This slide serves the dual purpose of reminding them that we can outperform (as recently as the fourth quarter) and also that the current environment continues to be difficult in general and even more so for a growth manager like us.

Slide 3:
This chart is prepared using third party software and helps support our case – that we are fundamentally a growth manager.

Slide 4:
Now I reinforce that we are a growth manager by showing how we did during a strong growth environment.

Slide 5:
This slide is an extension of the previous one. It provides more data about our performance during strong growth and value markets.

Slide 6:
Again a detailed look at growth versus value and our relative performance.

Slide 7:
Now I talk about the reason why our results have been weak. Although the extended period of outperformance by value managers is clear, it now appears to be in the process of reversing.

Slide 8:
Why do we persist in our belief in growth investing?

Slide 9:
But recent performance of these factors has been poor.

Slide 10:
Though not without precedent.

Slide 11:
Why do we think that growth is rebounding? This slide gives hope that our underperformance will reverse some time soon.

Slide 12:
We have been a model of consistency and outperformance over the longer term.

Slide 13:
A specific example.

Slide 14:
A summary of our philosophy and process. I put this in every presentation.

The balance of my presentation digs deeper into the portfolio structure. I end my presentation as I began – with a summary of the key points.

Regardless of how you choose to reach your clients – slides, e-mail, letters, telephone calls, face-to-face meetings, there are some do's and don'ts to keep in mind.

Some Do's

- Hold the client's hand (figuratively). Please remember, after handling your client, wash your hands.

- Treat people as individuals, not as abstract entities or target markets.

- Be assertive, confident and straightforward. Communicate good energy and positive feeling whenever possible. For example, you could remind the client about the specific circumstances and time period your investment style has tended to be out of favor and how you are confident the pendulum is about to swing the other way. Drop your "salesman's" bluster.

- Spend time crafting your story. Understand your presentation – know the details and be prepared to follow up on requests for supplementary information.

- Follow up with proof that answers client requests.

- Tell clients about any investment process or administrative enhancements you have made.

- Use all the human resources you have at your disposal. Your accounting nerd may resonate better than a sales personality during hard times with your clients. Also your personality may irritate them and if performance slips this may be the thing that pushes the client right over the edge.

- Try and meet with senior people in the client's organization who rarely attend your scheduled meetings. You did this initially to win the business. Or meet individually with the brightest or most interested on the client's finance committee to help them dig into the nitty gritty of your process and hopefully win their buy-in to what you do.

- Draw people out and identify their real concerns. Maybe they hate equities generally or the industry specifically, not you, your firm or the "bad" coffee you give them in meetings. Methodically and deliberately resolve their issues. If they are really uptight recommend anger management, aerobics and yoga.

Some Don'ts

- Don't lie or make excuses. At various times in my professional career, I have had to respond to negative feedback on the spot. For example, once, a performance measurement consultant presented my client's investment committee with a lengthy and damning portrait of the reasons for our poor investment performance. This resembled a dissection in high school biology class, and I was the slimy frog.

The consultant's analysis was detailed and right on the mark. When he had finished he left. The room was silent. I felt that everybody was waiting for my response.

I took a deep breath and said, "Well, that was very interesting" and all of my clients' heads nodded in agreement. "And," I continued, "To be frank, the consultant said so much I am not quite sure what to make of it all." To my delight all the clients' heads nodded again.

Suddenly I realized that their heads were nodding because they were sleeping. The consultant's long and boring presentation had put them into a coma! They hadn't heard a word he or I had said. He saved my neck!

Seriously, the lesson here is that I wasn't there to refute or make excuses for my poor performance.

- Don't seem stupid by saying things like, "The market is wrong."

- Don't blame others in your firm, like your portfolio manager!

- Don't rely on your portfolio manager to save you or even to explain good performance. Your portfolio manager is good at his or her job but not necessarily at explaining it, especially in lay language.

- Don't say you don't know – if you don't know who does? And by the way bring them along next time and don't forget to close the door on your way out!

- Don't send out new people when the results are weak. Your clients will feel abandoned.

- Don't rely on technology. Nothing beats a face-to-face meeting although the telephone and e-mails can be useful supplements.

- Don't rely on heavy drinking, big lunches and golf to get you through the tough spots. Just heavy drinking alone is enough. Seriously, this is the time to offer information and support. Simple, honest, useful dialogue is best.

- Don't bother your clients if you don't have anything useful to tell them.

- Don't ask for feedback on your website or your brochure – this isn't the time to be doing client surveys unless you want to call attention to your own lack of control.

When I first entered the industry, I was lucky enough to have a mentor. He was wildly successful – in good markets and in bad markets and in everything in between.

Over the years, my mentor told me things that saved me a lot of time, money and aggravation – when I bothered to listen to him. He once said that, "Sales people are the most overpaid people in the world in the good times and the most underpaid people in the world in the bad times."

He said that giving clients "good" news is easy. Giving them "bad" news is not. And, if you think for one minute that the client will continue to work with you if you don't communicate with them personally, professionally and promptly, think again!

Treat your clients the way you'd want to be treated when something goes wrong. Don't make excuses for your service or performance shortcomings. And if your knees shake and your heart rate speeds up, remember that's what Valium is for.

I will now take two or three questions from the audience.

Q1: A question I'm often asked is how the mutual fund market and the consulting market are different from the institutional market.

Q2: There is a fine line between being a client advocate and representing your firm's position. I'm often asked to define the difference between the two.

My final words to you are:

1. Get ready to earn your pay!

2. Meet with clients personally.

3. Don't send out new people when results are weak – your clients will feel abandoned.

4. Present performance numbers in context.

5. And during REALLY tough markets remember; keep your wits about you, your passport handy, your suitcase packed and your car running!"

Why the humor in this speech works

The humor in the speech humanizes the presenter and makes it easier for the audience to follow the long series of often boring facts. The humor keeps the audience focused as a collective, on select instances, which sell the presenter's arguments.

Example 2: HOW TO HIRE A MONEY MANAGER

Presented by the president of a money management firm to 75 people responsible for their company pension plans.

"When I was asked to talk about the qualities of a good Money Manager and the process involved in selecting one, the first thing that popped into my mind was, "That's easy, just make sure they don't have a criminal record. Now, how am I going to fill the other 44 minutes?" "No problem," I thought. "I'll start by talking about myself."

If you've had a chance to read my bio you know I am a Money Manager with XYZ Company and you may be wondering what one Money Manager can tell you about selecting others. In my professional career I have worked as a Consultant, and have listened to Money Managers tell me why they should be hired. I have even recommended some of them to my clients. I also spent a number of years as an Internal Pension Fund Manager and discovered that managing money is somewhat tougher than it looks from the outside as a Consultant.

My next step was working as a Portfolio Manager in a value shop where I received my basic training in the importance of sound fundamental analysis, buying things cheaply, and making sure I had the lowest interest rate available on my credit card. Fundamental analysis didn't always result in success – sometimes companies went bankrupt. It was however superb training.

For the last five years, I have worked in a growth shop. The most important lesson I have learned so far is the importance of managing risk.

So, the bottom line is, I have sat on all sides of the desk – as a Consultant, an Internal Pension Fund Manager, and then as a Money Manager, which is why you might find my perspective on the selection process both interesting and useful.

Over the next half hour or so I will discuss what I see as the two sides of the Money Manager selection equation; that is, from the perspective of the Pension Fund Sponsor and Consultant on the one hand, and from the Money Manager applicant on the other. Let's start with a review of some of the things we already know.

The Greenwich Survey recently reported that most major Consultants have more than five hundred Money Managers in their database. That's a lot of Money Managers to choose from. So, if you could eliminate some of my competitors, I'd really appreciate it!

Because there are so many candidates, sometimes it is extremely difficult for Pension Fund Sponsors and their Consultants to differentiate between them. Add staff turnover and changes in ownership to the mix and anyone would be hard-pressed to tell a Picasso from a Peanuts cartoon.

We all know that Pension Fund Sponsors and their Consultants should monitor Style Rotation. Remember how the technology sector contributed to strong performance by growth managers in the late nineties?

In the last couple of years, the market did an about-face and Value Investing regained popularity. And when we look at the stats from the last couple of months, the pendulum seems to have swung back to favor Growth Investing again.

For those of you with children, let me put it this way: remember when bell-bottoms were in? And then they were out? And now your kids are wearing them again? In other words, you have to look beyond the style to the substance within.

And most of us have begun to suspect that Index Funds may not provide the answer either. Just look at the problems encountered by indices with large stock weightings in specific sectors. It wasn't that long ago that the IT sector represented almost thirty percent of the S&P 500 Index and the overall index became heavily tilted towards Growth.

Bill Miller, a well-regarded U.S. Money Manager, recently suggested the S&P 500 Index is just another Actively Managed portfolio. Miller notes that the people who decide on the Index don't limit stock or industry weightings, prefer large cap over small cap and yes, their turnover is low. These built-in tendencies suggest Index Funds may not be as safe as one might assume. This makes sense. If technology stocks are doing well and the Index is heavily tilted towards Growth, the Money Manager who does not buy technology stocks will not perform as well as the Index, which favors those stocks.

If we look at Canadian bonds and the U.S. equity market in particular, adding value through active management isn't always a slam-dunk either. That is not to say there isn't an opportunity for adding value in these two asset classes, it's just that some extra effort and care is required in reviewing style and selecting a Money Manager.

Finally, many companies rely on Consultants to help them select the "best" Money Manager. And, there are many talented Consultants out there. Unfortunately, many of them move on to other things, which means a tremendous knowledge resource is lost each year. Don't believe me?

Just think of talented people like Wendy Brodkin, Bill Solomon, and Audrey Robinson from Towers Perrin, many of the people from SEI, Harry Marmer from Willliam M. Mercer, John Ilkiw from Frank Russell who are all no longer Consultants in Canada.

The point is that all of these outstanding Consultants have moved on to other activities. Even consulting firms like SEI and Frank Russell have shifted their focus from pure consulting to Manager-of-Manager Products. With these products Consultants change their business model to generate revenues from an hourly fee basis to a percentage of assets.

To summarize:

- There are lots of qualified Money Managers but staff turnover and changes in ownership may affect performance.

- Style rotation should be monitored carefully.

- Index funds offer a ready, but not risk-free solution.

- And Consultant turnover affects the quality of decision-making by Pension Fund Sponsors.

With this historical review in mind, let's begin our tour by looking at Money Manager selection from the perspective of the Pension Fund Sponsor and their Consultant.

First, we tend to rely on performance numbers. However, the numbers themselves do not provide a complete picture. Good performance numbers may simply mean that the Money Manager caught a wave that was due anyway because their investment style matched one that was currently in favor. Sometimes, this makes it difficult to determine if good performance results from skill or luck.

Speaking of which, there is a famous story about a Hungarian military unit on maneuvers in the Alps that got caught in a severe snowstorm. On the third day, the storm stopped and the soldiers returned to base camp.

When asked to explain what took them so long, the soldiers told their base commander that one of the soldiers found a map in his pocket. When the snowstorm stopped they just followed the map back to base camp.

The commanding officer asked to see map. To his astonishment it was not a map of the Alps, but a map of the Pyrenees. Instead of telling his men this little detail, he figured that since it had worked for them once, it would probably keep on working...so he gave the soldiers their new marching orders, handed them back their map and sent them on their way. P.S. They're still looking for them.

The point of this story is this: although luck might get you there the first time, I wouldn't book any mountain vacations based on that.

When numbers are readily available, people tend to rely on statistics to assess risk. They review performance in terms of upside/downside ratio, sharp ratio, information ratio, and so on. As a result, short-term performance numbers have become particularly relied upon, given people's short-term memories. In my opinion, performance numbers are unreliable and frankly, unstable, because as time passes, numbers change, styles change, people change and so on. In my opinion, there isn't enough emphasis placed on People, Process and the Money Manager's Personality and Investment Style.

Something else to consider is that Consultants often provide the information about performance and people. But who measures the Consultant's performance in their ability to recommend outstanding Money Managers? In Australia for example, they bring in a third party who actually measures this. And no, the third party isn't the Crocodile Hunter, even if the Consultants in Australia can be as mean as crocodiles about having their own advice measured.

Hiring a Money Manager is not the same thing as hiring an employee. Since market changes are reflected in portfolios every second, most Money Managers are under incredible pressure to deliver good results just that quickly.

Imagine what it would be like to have your personal work performance objectively measured daily, weekly, monthly and quarterly against people with a similar function to yours across Canada. Then your boss would regularly review what quartile you are in and would fire you if you were below average.

Contrast this with the rules governing employee performance, which is reviewed privately and is not published on the internet or in the daily newspapers for everyone in the country to see. If employee performance was assessed in the same way, the business world would be continually in court defending itself against employee Human Rights Violation charges.

Another issue with Money Manager selection involves presentations. Short-listed candidates are rarely interviewed for more than one half-hour to an hour. Yet, as any Human Resources Department worth its salt will attest, single interviews are notoriously unreliable. If we conduct many separate interviews before we hire one senior employee, why do we only allow one hour to interview someone who will be responsible for the financial health and security of all of our employees? That's like letting someone drive your Formula

One racecar after a spin around the parking lot in a golf cart!

One could argue that while both the Pension Fund Sponsor and the Bagel Baker need to separate the wheat from the chaff, it is far more difficult for the Pension Fund Sponsor. It takes time to understand the style, scope and abilities of each candidate. In my experience, two few Pension Fund Sponsors are willing to make the investment.

Here's what I mean. At XYZ Company we often have Consultants and Pension Fund prospects visit our offices, for a thorough 'due diligence' visit. These visits typically last anywhere from a half-day to as long as two full business days. Meetings involve a wide variety of people from our analytical departments, including portfolio management, risk management, performance measurement, compliance and business strategy. Contrast this with the typical one-hour interview in the Pension Sponsor's boardroom.

It's also interesting to note that, if three short-listed candidates present at 9:00 a.m., 10:00 a.m. and 11 a.m., sixty percent of the time, the candidate who presented at 9:00 a.m. will get the job. The evidence for this comes from research conducted by a company that advises Money Managers on presentation skills. So, if the Consultant tells me to, "Be there at 9:00 a.m." I can safely tell my wife to go ahead and book that Bermuda getaway.

Presentations that focus on brand can be particularly influential on Selection Committees. This is a problem when the Committee has limited or only occasional money management experience The strength of the "brand" becomes an unstated "performance guarantee," which some Selection Committees find reassuring.

Money Managers know this. That is why many presentations focus on their brand and important "facts" like their company has two hundred years of experience, and that their great-grandfather on their mother's side was Benjamin Graham and on their father's side was Benjamin Franklin. What salespeople neglect to tell you is that their two hundred years of experience comes from ten twenty year old employees and that the closest their great–grandfather came to Benjamin Franklin was owning a U.S. $100 bill.

So what have we got so far? Traditionally, Pension Fund Sponsors have relied on recent performance numbers and the Consultant's advice and brand. As I've already suggested and as I will explain further, this results in sub-optimal decision-making, or as they like to call it in the candy business, "fudging up big-time!" And now, my least favorite part, I'd like to discuss how Money Managers contribute to the problem.

First, I believe some Money Managers spend far too much time and money making sure their relationship with the different Consultants is very, very strong.

Their salespeople really start the dog and pony show when they are short-listed for a presentation, because that's when they get the chance to walk on their hind legs and speak. Presentations are always tailored to appeal to Selection Committee member interests, tastes and biases.

The presenters themselves are often assertive even aggressive and are confident and experienced. Remember that they have more experience in selling than most Committees have in buying. Finally, Money Managers try to be the first presenter for the reasons mentioned earlier. The obvious question is, "If you are the Pension Sponsor, how does any of this work in your favor?" The obvious answer is, it doesn't.

You have to know the person you are hiring, not just what the sales people emphasize. In order to do that you have to realize that when it comes to Money Managers, there are personality styles and there are investment styles.

It goes without saying that all Money Mangers are smart, although as my wife always tells me, some are smarter than others. In terms of personality, value managers are generally stable and reserved, while fixed income mangers are probably the most conservative and cautious. Growth managers, on the other hand, tend to be more extraverted, assertive, even flamboyant, and are often quite good presenters. Given this, what type of Money Manager do you think would give the best interview?

I would respectfully suggest that the quality of the presentation, whether by sales people or the Money Manager is completely irrelevant. It is far more relevant to assess the character of each Money Manager candidate, their personal investing style, their personality style, and their obsession with investing.

I believe outstanding Money Managers become successful first, because of their ability to select securities and second because of their obsession with investing.

As for my second point, obsession with investing is a positive characteristic in managing money. As a matter of fact, I have it on good authority that Money Management is the only profession where having an obsessive/compulsive disorder is a competitive advantage!

The only problem with having an obsessive Money Manager is that he or she can become pathological which reminds me of a mental health clinic on Bay Street that only treated Money Managers.

One day, the clinic advertised for a Money Manager for its pension fund. Unfortunately for them, they short-listed three of their own patients who were under heavy medication.

They asked the first candidate, "What's two plus two?" Candidate #1 answered, "Thursday, Friday, Saturday." They asked the second candidate the same question. He also said, "Thursday, Friday, Saturday."

When they asked the third candidate the question, were they ever surprised when the candidate answered "Four." So, they asked the third candidate how he came up with "Four." He said, "Because I realized that I would need Thursday, Friday, Saturday and Sunday to get the answer."

Let's just take a few moments to look at how investment style affects performance results. To do this we need to agree on a definition for each style. Unfortunately, that's not easy. For example, in the international market, the MSCI Index focuses on price-to-book to define style whereas Salomon Smith Barney Indices use a wider variety of characteristics to define value and growth stocks. Luckily, both of them agree on the importance of the kind of car you drive. Just kidding.

To further complicate the discussion, Money Managers tend to have somewhat mixed styles and it is neither easy nor advisable to typecast them. On a related note, although many Value Management styles are similar, there appears to be more investment styles amongst Growth Managers.

Let me explain. Because of their emphasis on price, virtually all Value Managers tend to buy stocks that are trading at:

- low price to book
- or low price sales
- or low price cash flow
- or low price earnings

and such stocks tend to be highly correlated in the market place because price is the common factor in all of these ratios.

On the other hand, Growth Managers may choose to emphasize different characteristics such as stock price momentum, forecast sales growth or historic earnings growth. However, because stock price, company sales and earnings have a low degree of correlation with each other, Growth Managers may choose to emphasize different characteristics and their results may differ enormously.

So it's not like comparing McDonald's managers and Burger King managers, which would be relatively simple. It's more like comparing bank managers with Burger King managers, which is why it is more difficult to assess the merits of any particular style in a one-hour interview.

It's also worth mentioning that recent academic evidence suggests that the more a Money Manager adheres to one investment style, the more likely it is the Manager will outperform his or her peers in the future – something to keep in mind when researching Money Manager candidates.

To briefly recap, Fund Manager selection can be a heck of a lot easier when you understand the landscape. I've talked about various issues ranging from Investment styles to personality styles and how relying on the traditional interview process alone is a risky proposition and why. I would now like to make some concrete suggestions on how to improve your search results, and incidentally to become a better parent. Six P's can help guide us along the way.

The First P: Preparation

- Thorough preparation is essential.

- Determine your appetite for risk.

- Review and understand your personal biases.

- Study all of the material you have received from your Consultants.

- Remember to consider your own experience.

- Get an advance copy of the Money Manager's presentation.

The Second P: Person

- Get to know the person who will be responsible for achieving your objectives.

- Carefully review Money Manager turnover and changes of control and for the impact this has had on performance.

- Do your due diligence investigation before the final presentation. Undertake a site visit.

- During the presentation, be consciously aware of your bias in favor of the first presenter.

The Third P: Presentation

- Don't be seduced by a slick presentation.

- The best Money Manager may be the worst presenter.

The Fourth P: Perspective

- Try to maintain your perspective.

- Ask yourself how much of the Manager's performance, whether good or bad, is a result of his or her investment style.

- Articulate your concerns. For example, are you concerned about short-term risk or should you be thinking about long-term risk and long-term return? Figure this out in advance!

The Fifth P: Persistent

- Dig for answers.

- Talk to ex-clients, but remember that an ex-client may be like an ex-spouse.

My Sixth P is really a P.S.

Do your best to ignore the Money Manager's stated philosophy. For the most part, this is a marketing invention.

In conclusion, I encourage you to work very hard at making sure the hiring process works to your advantage and that you get what you want – long-term outstanding performance from your Money Manager.

Unravel the mystery of the selection process. Without a clear, unbiased approach to Money Manager Selection your investment returns are at risk.

And remember, even a worm looks good to a sardine. If your process for Money Manager Selection is deficient, you will probably have to swallow poor performance, and like the sardine, run a big risk of being canned!"

Why the humor in this speech works

Once again, a long, intellectually complex narrative is enlivened by even very occasional bouts of humor. The audience is more willing to go along with the presenter if they see him or her as a wit that can add some passion in the form of laughter to the discourse. As well, as the jokes are really off subject, there is some relief at letting go the complex "facts" for a moment before returning to the presentation at hand.

Example 3: AFTER DINNER ENTERTAINMENT

Script for a comedy show for the after-dinner entertainment of about 75 financial advisors from the same company, both men and women.

"I hope all of you are having a good time at the conference. From the looks of things, the people who run things have gone to great lengths to make your experience here educational, comfortable, and even pleasurable.

You take care of other people's lives and are to be congratulated. Because you handle their money. I'm sure many of your clients are taken back to their teenage years when their parents controlled the cash. I wonder whether any of your clients occasionally ask if they can borrow your car on Saturday night?

Unfortunately I get no financial support from my own family. In fact, only six months ago I was so broke that I wanted to move back in with my parents. But, they had just moved back in with their parents!

And now I hear that as of January first, the Ontario government is going to start testing for drugs in the workplace. That seems stupid to me. Work is such a depressing experience that never mind testing for drugs in the workplace, they should be GIVING drugs to people in the workplace! A little Ecstasy in the water cooler and nobody would care about RRSP season!

XYZ advisors do estate planning. Very important work. I tried to do my own estate planning a few years ago. It didn't work out very well. I joined a pre-paid funeral plan where you pay for your funeral in advance in installments. Just my luck,

I was laid off work and I couldn't keep up the payments. Now I have to die twelve years earlier. I hate it when that happens!

I've done a lot of research on your company through the internet and I'm learning a lot more about XYZ company. For example, I learned your company name was inspired by The Lion King movie and it means "Thank you" in Swahili. Strangely enough, in Bantu it means, "Trust me, I know more than you do."

I think I read that many of you make a lot of your money from trailer fees and I couldn't help thinking, "Wow, one really good tornado and they're wiped out."

Apparently, fiduciary responsibility is quite important and as a matter of fact, I've just decided to become more responsible in my own life. From now on, I'm not letting the convenience store lotto machine pick my 649 numbers. I'm choosing them myself!

Going through your website I was surprised to see that XYZ also provides services to many of the professional football players in the National Football League – career management, contract negotiations, and bailing half of them out of jail. In fact, I hear that next year, XYZ company is sponsoring a new football award – "Most Yards Gained in a Single Police Pursuit."

Managing athletes must be the most difficult job of all. For example, so many international athletes have failed their drug tests recently that they should seriously think of changing the name to the "World Crack and Field Championships."

Actually, they should have a World Crack and Field Championship. It would be exciting. Get a bunch of crack addicts, take their crack away from them, put just enough crack at the finish line for one person and let 'em go. You'd see some desperate finishing kicks! And what about the stabbings!

I used to teach university in Montreal and in some ways you remind me of my former students. Many of you are asleep, some people are still eating their lunch and I know you will applaud enthusiastically when I finish because you can't wait to rush outside and have a smoke.

So, goodbye and thank you for being so appreciative, and not throwing things at me, like money, because true riches come to us in the form of the love and respect we garner from others, and checks and bearer bonds from people whose names I can't mention but you know who they are.

Remember that laughter is the best medicine, unless you're sick, in which case you shouldn't have moved to Florida."

Why the humor in this speech works

The humor in this speech is more pronounced than in a typical business speech, but still works well to humanize both the speaker and the object of the humor and to render the audience more affectionate toward both. The sharp wit is impressive on several levels and shores up the rationale for accepting the presenter's points .

Example 4: SUZEN FROMSTEIN'S FIVE-MINUTE TOASTMASTERS HUMOROUS SPEECH CONTEST ENTRY

Presented to about 125 business people.

"How many of you were born married?

OK, how many of you ever needed a date?

I recently started dating again. I only did it because of LSD – low sex drive. Listen it's better than NSD – no sex drive.

I had been in a committed, monogamous relationship for so long, I didn't know what I should do or where I should go to meet a new man.

So, I went where I always go when I need some good advice. I went to my daddy. Would you believe he told me to focus on raising my kids?

Visits that lasted a couple of hours a week did not qualify a doting grandfather as an expert on my kids, Search and Destroy.

So I did what every loving daughter does – I ignored his advice.

Maybe some positive affirmations might work.

So, every morning before I got up I stood in front of the mirror and said, "I am a magnet for romance. Males find me irresistible."

And, I got a lot of positive response too – from the dog.

What would you have done to get some current dating information?

I bought Modern Romance, True Confessions and National Lampoon magazines. But I got so many mixed messages I needed mental floss to clear the plaque from my mind.

One night, while I was on a romantic walk (with the dog) it suddenly occurred to me that a businesslike approach to dating just might work.

You network when you do a job search. I could apply these same skills in my search for romance.

I ran home and pulled up my contact list. I called all my friends and colleagues who might have leads.

I told them I would consider any man, even if he had five previous marriages, 27 kids and wore platform shoes.

While I was waiting for my network to kick in, I decided to spruce up my image. I cut my bangs. I plucked my eyebrows. I dyed a few grey hairs.

I also joined a dating service. I was impressed with the scientific way it approached the matter. I signed up for 18 men – just playing the odds.

My first date finally called and we agreed to meet. I arrived at the appointed place, but there must have been some mistake.

He said he had brown hair. He should have said brown head with hair on the side.

And, Prince Charming was so pale and pathetically thin I could lift him up and carry him across the threshold.

I wanted a man and they sent me a chicken. If I wanted a chicken, I could have ordered KFC, and it would have been cheaper too. I asked for my money back.

Daddy suggested I place an ad in the local business papers. Since I always take everything he says with a grain of salt, I picked Playboy. (Stage direction: I opened a copy of a Playboy magazine I was using as a prop and pretended to read from It).

"Sexy. Spontaneous and Self-Supporting Single Woman, Seeks Like-Minded Gentleman. I am 110 lbs. of passion. I won the 2009 Miss Wet T- Shirt Contest. (They didn't have to know it was from my kids dribbling all over me). Experienced only need apply."

I sat back and waited for the flood of emails I was sure I was going to get. In total I received ten replies. The first was from a woman. She needed a baby-sitting job.

The other nine were from unemployed accountants. "Self-supporting" seems to be the only word any of them picked up on.

Luckily by this time my network kicked in.

I dated older men, who said they wanted to meet a 'grown up' woman. But they all left me for the nubile valley girl types with teenaged minds.

So I switched. I dated younger men who said they appreciated a stable and mature woman like me. But they also left me for the well endowed, and I'm talking 'big' bucks, golden girl type.

I started to wonder if men got whiplash from changing their minds.

Then the unexpected happened. I met someone and he actually satisfied some of my criteria. He's single. He's male. He's a sexologist.

He also has 27 kids – he drives a bus.

He had five previous marriages – he's got references.

And he's shorter than I am – he looks up to me.

The way I see it, there is only one major stumbling block.

How am I ever going to tell daddy that I'm dating Dr. Ruth?"

Why the humor in this speech works

I first asked, "How many of you were born married?" Since, that question was obviously an absurdity, I had the attention of the audience. My follow up question told the audience what my speech was about, "OK, how many of you ever needed a date?" These two short questions forced the audience to consider my premise. Then it was time to confirm what my speech was about. "I recently started dating again. I only did it because of LSD – low sex drive. Listen it's better than NSD – no sex drive." That is how I established context, rapport and laughter in the first thirty seconds, which is essential for a humorous speech.

BIOS

Meet Suzen Fromstein

Want to Inform, Influence and Entertain Like a Pro? Simply Recognize The Seven Deadly Sins of Public Speaking And Then Avoid Them is Suzen's second book. Suzen made her debut as a published author with SUITS AND LADDERS: Ten Proven Ways to Keep Your Job Safe (with a few jokes thrown in).

This Amazon (Career and Career Guides) Best Selling Book consolidates the combined wisdom of 102 real people with real jobs. Following their advice gives employees (regardless of industry or sector) a better chance of survival, or at least, gives them a fighting chance at survival.

Forever the optimist, Suzen swears Killers, Coffins & Cadavers, a comedy e-book on death and dying co-authored with stand-up comic Michael Nemiroff and comedic actress Elaine Smookler will be published at some point - whether in this lifetime or the next remains to be seen. Until then she will continue to speak and write about more mundane subjects like career, relationships and the rapport-building power of laughter.

In addition to writing books, Suzen is the high priestess and sole proprietor of her own business communications firm, The Write Connections Inc. and specializes in the deathly-difficult task of making business communications humorous.

Suzen regularly tweets (@LaughLogic) wisdom from SUITS AND LADDERS and Want to Inform, Influence and Entertain Like a Pro?

Meet Michael Nemiroff

Michael Nemiroff began his performing career by teaching English literature to teenagers at Montreal's Concordia University. He always refers to this as, "Trying to teach the principles of vegetarianism to alligators." In 1998, Michael decided to leave academia for the more financially rewarding world of stand-up comedy.

Since then, he has crisscrossed North America, playing gigs at clubs, hotels, bars, restaurants, army bases, wedding chapels, bowling alleys and taco stands. Along the way, Michael has performed with comedy stars such as Norm MacDonald, Dave Attell and Jon Stuart. Michael has written jokes for other comics (sometimes without realizing it) and has contributed comedy material to The Tonight Show With Jay Leno, so there.

Michael doesn't take himself or the rest of you very seriously and has developed a reputation for clever, offbeat humor, mostly at the expense of others. Doing professional stand-up comedy for over a decade has left Michael with the satisfaction of having brought laughter to dozens of people, a limp, and the belief that the moon is trying to kill him.